READY REFERENCE TO REVOLUTIONARIES
(A GUIDE TO ACTION)

READY REFERENCE TO REVOLUTIONARIES (A GUIDE TO ACTION)

V.T. Rajshekar

GYAN

ISBN : 978-81-212-1287-8

First Published, 2015

Published by

Gyan Publishing House
23, Main Ansari Road, Darya Ganj,
New Delhi- 110 002
Ph. : 2328 2060, 2326 1060
E-mail: books@gyanbooks.com

Printed at : Reliable Infomedia, New Delhi

Cataloging in Publication Data—DK
Courtesy: D.K. Agencies (P) Ltd. <docinfo@dkagencies.com>

Rajshekar Shetty, V. T., 1932- **author.**
Ready reference to revolutionaries : a guide to action / V.T. Rajshekar.
pages cm
Reprint.
ISBN 9788121212878

1. Brahmanism. 2. Dalits—India—Social conditions. 3. Human rights—India. I. Title.

DDC 294.5 23

THE AUTHOR

FOREWORD FOR THE SECOND REVISED EDITION

India is fast becoming a sick country and a failed state. Every prediction made in *Dalit Voice* has come true. It is also becoming ungovernable. This is because the country's destitute and deprived population (about 30%) – "wretched of the earth" – is simply forgotten. Another 30 to 35% are struggling for survival.

Only a mere 15% of the upper castes are counted and their voice is called "public opinion". The rulers are carrying on "governing" the country projecting a false picture painted by the highly prejudiced Brahminical media. We call it toilet papers.

Yet the country is not collapsing because the rulers have mastered two tricks:

(1) Keep the destitutes divided, instigating one ("Hindus") against the other (Muslim), and thus making the brothers fight brothers.

(2) The destitutes comprising mainly the Dalits, Tribals and Backward Castes (a total of 65%) are brainwashed to believe that they are Hindu and then injected the deadliest Hindu poison into their blood. The job is done.

This gigantic Hindu tentacle has reached every nook and corner of India and with the power of its temples manned by crafty Brahmin priests, it can mesmerise every "Hindu" and make him/her believe that he/she is suffering because of their own crimes committed in the previous birth (*karma*) and such sins can be washed by propitiating the god (meaning the godman). The destitute is now convinced that he himself is the cause of his suffering. This centuries-old deathless Hindu counter-revolutionary machine that is making the destitute totally impotent, lifeless and controlling their social and cultural life is more powerful than and above the country's constitutionally established government.

So much so the deprived destitutes (65%) are unable even able to identify their oppressor — not to speak of rising in revolt.

How then a revolution is possible in India when Hinduism has made the very slave to enjoy his slavery?

Yet with all these obstacles, Dalit movement — India's only revolutionary movement — is managing to make some headway.

This *Ready Reference* is enlarged and further strengthened as a guide to action to our people.

Bangalore, India

Jan. 1, 2007 ***V.T. Rajshekar***

FOREWORD FOR THE FIRST EDITION

India's Dalit movement is coming of age despite all the oppression it faces daily. The ruling upper castes have all the wealth, glamour, positions, posts and privileges with them. More than that they have the state power so that they can persecute us "lawfully". The oppression and persecution has increased manifold particularly after "independence" (1947).

And the country's "national press" is working overtime to see that the oppressed Untouchables, Tribals, Backward Castes on one side and the religious "minorities" (Muslim/Christian/Sikhs) remain deprived and distressed.

But the very weight of the oppressed population, comprising over 85% of the country's 1,000-million population, is chilling the bone marrow of the oppressors who out of their anger and frustration are committing blunders after blunders helping our people.

The latest is the violent upper caste racist war (1990) against the Mandal Commission Report which recommended reservation (human rights) to Backward Castes forming 35% of the population of India. This war woke up many of the sleeping slaves of India. And this brought us hundreds of queries and we are made to answer them.

A Brahmin journalist interviewed us at Mangalore and it was taped. The following is the interview.

Bangalore, India

Jan.1, 1991

V.T. Rajshekar

Ready Reference to Revolutionaries

Introduction:

In our day-to-day work, all revolutionaries in India are confronted with certain intricate questions, perplexing puzzles, difficult situations which as followers of Dr. Babasaheb Ambedkar, we are called upon to solve. We cannot ignore these questions trying to pretend that they will be solved automatically or as the movement mounts. As leaders of both thought and action, the Ambedkarites have to tackle them and decide them then and there and once for all. Otherwise, it will be a grievous tactical error. And one error may lead to bigger error.

Misunderstanding and malice, arrogance and suspicion have long been the bane of revolutionaries. Dog eating dog is a daily feature. So, some common questions put to us at different places plus a taped interview are posed here and answers given to guide revolutionaries. Why we give so much of importance to Ambedkarites and not anybody else is because as Ambedkarites — genuine and dedicated followers and experts on the thoughts of Dr. Babasaheb Ambedkar — they will be the natural leaders of Indian Revolution.

Every other movement is dead in India today. Gandhian movement, marxist movement, naxalite movement, JP movement, Periyar movement, Lohia movement, Sri Narayana Guru movement are all dead. The only movement that has not only survived but taken an all-

India role, much feared and respected, is the Ambedkarite (Dalit) movement. So our Ambedkarites have the greatest responsibility of liberating all the oppressed *Anaryan* (non-Hindu) original inhabitants of India, amounting to over 85% of its population. We call them *Bahujans* (majority population). Hence these questions and answers are addressed to Ambedkarites.

Admission to Brahmins

Q. Should we allow the Brahmins to join the Dalit movement ?

A: Brahmins as the chief promoters of caste system, which is the other name for Hinduism, cannot be **trusted** for the time being. Because the moment they join our movement, Dalits will be displaced and Brahmins will take control of all Dalit organisations. We have nothing against individual Brahmins. In fact, we are not against anybody. If Brahmins want to support us — whatever be its shape — we will accept it but we cannot allow them to enter our organisation. They can come only as our servants. (*Dalit Voice*, Editorial July 16, 2005: "*Mayawati follows good old dictum: Brahmins are bad masters but good servants*").

Gandhi & nonviolence

Q: What is your attitude to M.K. Gandhi, his gandhism and his nonviolence?

A: The answer is given in our book, *Hinduism, Fascism & Gandhism* (Dalit Sahitya Akademy, DSA-1985). We don't like anybody pretending to be nonviolent and turn-the-other-cheekish. Nonviolence is nonsense. Nonviolence is the language of the cowards. We don't see how any revolution can be nonviolent. I have never heard of a nonviolent revolution or a revolution that was brought about by turning the other cheek (did Christ say that?). And so it is a crime for anyone to teach a person, who is the victim of violence, to continue to be nonviolent without doing something to teach himself self-defence. Remember, self-defence is no violence. Self-defence is resistance — resisting the violent enemy. If this is what gandhism teaches, then it is a criminal philosophy from the point of the victims of violence. That is why, we have said gandhism is nothing but sugar-coated counter-revolution.

Q: Does it mean we have to reject non-violence?

A: No. Our people, Dalits and all other oppressed people of India, are the most non-violent people on earth. As the original inhabitants of India, they are the producers of the country's entire wealth. Producers of wealth anywhere in the world are never violent. It is always the consumers of wealth who are violent. However, we are non-violent only with non-violent people. I can remain non-violent as long as you are also non-violent. But you can't ask me to be non-violent after punching my face. Do you want me to be silent when you rape my sister before my very eyes?

Budha never preached nonviolence

The right of the people to seek arms for self-defence shall not be curbed. Dalits don't realise that they are within their constitutional rights to keep a knife, axe. Or even a gun if you can afford. Purely for self-defence.

Because for centuries only Dalits have been victims of violence. So they have a right to self-defence.

As India is a state ruled by our Brahminical oppressors, who are with their fully armed military, police and other paramilitary forces, they can unleash state terrorism on us. It is happening daily in all villages and cities — aided and abetted by the Brahminical judiciary and media. When our enemy is armed so recklessly, should we not possess at least a simple weapon ?

Dalits, the original inhabitants, have been always pacifist. Non-violent. So, nobody need advise us to be non-violent. It doesn't need a Gandhi. Dr. Ambedkar says:

> The Buddha has nowhere given any definition of *Ahimsa*. ... It is quite clear that Buddha meant to make a distinction between **will to kill and need to kill**. He did not ban killing where there was need to kill. What he banned was killing where there was nothing but the will to kill. (Dr. B.R. Ambedkar, *Buddha & His Dhamma*, W&S Vol.11, 1992, p.346).

Parliamentary democracy

Q: Can the problem of caste system in India be solved under India's existing parliamentary democracy ?

A: No. It can't. That doesn't mean we are against democracy. We are only against the existing Brahminical parliamentary democracy. And parliamentary democracy is not the only form of democracy known to the world. Caste system is the other word for Hinduism. It means if caste system has to be solved, Hinduism has to go.

Since parliamentary democracy cannot kill caste system,

we have to revive Dr. Ambedkar's proposal for separate electorate.

Problem of poverty

Q: Can there be any revolutionary change in India while the hostility between Dalits and the other "poor" exists? Can Dalits defend themselves alone without the support of other co-sufferers like Muslims, Sikhs and Christians?

A: Stop dividing people into "rich" and "poor". There are no "rich" or "poor" Indians. What we have is "upper" and "lower" castes. There may be some "poor" among Brahmins but these "poor" have been as much against not only the "poor" Dalits but all Dalits. Because to a Hindu all Dalits, "rich or poor", are hostile to his caste-based religion. Even the richest Dalit —Jagjivan Ram — was ill-treated. There can be no solidarity of the "poor" in India. It is simply not possible.

Serpent & mongoose can't co-exist

In India, the 15% Aryans constitute a separate race and the rest of the 85% are non-Aryans (non-Hindu) or *Anaryans*. So the non-Hindu people, the SC/ST/BCs (Scheduled Castes, Scheduled Tribes and Backward Castes) and Muslim/Christian/Sikh solidarity is the urgent need. The non-Hindus will never agree for "unity and integration" with the Aryans because they are our oppressors from centuries. The current unrest and consequent decay of this country is due to the fact that the Hindu rulers are making all their plans and "development schemes" to "integrate" our people with Hindus. How can oil and water mix? How can the serpent and mongoose co-exist?

As regards your question of "poor", I have already said there are no "poor" people in India. Dalits are kicked, killed, burnt and raped not because they are "poor" but because they are not willing to become part of the Hindu caste system. So too with the Muslims. A "poor" Muslim is not touched — only when he becomes "rich" he invites the wrath of the Hindu terrorists.

Marxists

Q: Can Dalits achieve their freedom without the help of progressive Hindus, particularly the marxists?

A: These "Hindu marxists" are more dangerous than Hindu nazi terrorists. I have elaborated this in my book, *How Marx Failed in Hindu India?* (DSA–1986).

The upper castes (Hindus) must know that it is the Dalits who built this house in which the Hindus are living. They built all the dams, they developed all the forests, they produced all the food, they constructed all the buildings, they laid all the roads, they made all the furniture. They are the producers of wealth and the upper castes are the consumers of wealth. The Hindus do not work. They sit, eat and manipulate things to exploit. This is happening because the consumers of wealth are made to think for us. We are the doers and they are the thinkers. This dichotomy must end.

How can it end? It can end only when the doers become thinkers. We can become thinkers only when we all get "educated" in the thoughts of Babasaheb. "Educate, Agitate, Organise", said Babasaheb in his "Three Commandments".

We have nothing against marxism as such because we

are born marxists. Our complaint is against India's upper caste marxists who have captured this maoist, marxist, naxalite parties and are using these parties to further enslave us. Maoists and naxalites of the world must support us to capture these parties.

Bogus human rightswalas

Q: What do you think of our human rights organisations? PUCL, PUDR etc. ?

A: Our human rights movement, less said the better about them. It is again dominated by Brahmins and other upper castes. They are all consumers of wealth. Only "thinkers". They think for us and we become the foot soldiers for their human rights movement. And they get away with all the awards and rewards. Did any SC/ST/BC or Muslim/Sikh or Christian get any human rights award in India? They enjoy at our cost. Our human rightswalas have not improved our human rights a wee bit in the course of last 60 years.

Our contention is these Hindu (upper caste) "liberals", "progressives" — we call them "Socialist Brahmins" — infiltrated the civil rights, human rights movement and took the Dalits for a ride.

We must kick out these human rightswalas. And if this is not possible, we must form our own human rights movement. We must refuse to be their drivers.

Anti-poverty schemes

Q: The Govt. of India has done so much for the welfare of Dalits. So many billions and billions of rupees have been spent on their welfare.

A: SC/ST/BCs are the indigenous peoples. They are the original inhabitants of India. But the upper caste writers have written false history saying that we are the "weaker sections of the Hindu society". This is false. Does history say that we are "Hindu"? What does our Saviour say? He said the Untouchables are not Hindu and were never Hindu. He said the Untouchables are a separate element. Once this fact is admitted and the UN Human Rights Commission is told about it, we will be entitled to international protection.

India's problem is not poverty

But India has not yet signed the Covenant on Human Rights. As for the billions and billions of rupees spent on our "welfare", I don't know where it went. The upper caste stomach anyway is bulging. The govt. is treating our problem as a problem of poverty. But our problem is not poverty. What we are asking for is our human rights. But they are pouring money to remove our non-existing poverty. If our people are "poor", it is because this poverty is the by-product of our deprivation. The moment we recover our lost rights—posts, privileges, power —we become "rich" automatically. The upper caste rulers also know this. So to deny us our human rights, they are trying to cure the symptom but not the disease. This is what we call the black heart. They know the disease. They also know that the medicine is available — but they are deliberately making a wrong diagnosis. Does it not prove their black heart?

You will get better idea on "our poverty" from our book, *Development Redefined* (DSA-2006).

India & South Africa

Q: The Indian Govt. is a champion of South African Blacks and invited Nelson Mandela in 1990 and conferred the highest title on him. What do you say?

A: Our upper caste rulers were in the forefront of anti-Apartheid movement but when it comes to the Apartheid at home, the worst in the world, they forward a false plea. Refer to what happened at Durban where the Hindus opposed us. Under the Brahminical religion, preaching need not have any connection with practice.

These upper castes shed tears on Apartheid but simultaneously practice the world's worst form of Apartheid inside India. The ruling religion of India, Hinduism, is itself a racist religion. In fact, racism originated in India.

Partition of India

Q: Do you welcome the partition (1947) of India?

A: The partition of India and Pakistan was a grave error. The upper caste (Hindu) leaders, led by M.K. Gandhi, conspired to divide India. The Hindu fear was if the Muslims remained in the undivided India, they would side with the SC/ST/BCs, and the upper castes would be isolated and reduced to a minority.

Partition was a Brahmin conspiracy. We must undo this partition so that we may solve many of our problems ourselves. We are for *Akhand Bharat* (which was once a Hindu nazi slogan —now forgotten) meaning uniting Pakistan and Bangladesh back with India. Are the Hindu nazis ready?

Are you a hate-monger ?

Q: Your critics say you are fanning hatred and your writings are polemical. What do you say?

A: Right. Some upper caste critics say that we are fanning hatred. They have to say that. They say I am instigating violence. But please note: to this day not a single Dalit has attacked an upper caste (Hindu) after hearing my speeches or reading my writings. So, the charge is baseless. On the other hand, the upper caste violence against SC/ST/BCs and minorities is going on unabated. It is increasing daily. (DV March 16, 2006 p.24: "*In defence of polemics*").

We are the victims of violence and many govt. reports and documents have said this. How can the victims of violence be accused of being violent? I can't understand this logic. A Hindu believes what he wants to believe. If he wants to believe that I am instigating violence, I can't help it. To this day no court in India has convicted me.

On the other hand, I was the victim of Hindu violence. I was arrested under the Terrorist Act (TADA) and put in the Chandigarh jail, my passport was impounded for 20 long years (in 2005 it was revoked).

"*Savarna* homeland"

I am not blood thirsty. I am one of India's millions of Dalits who is tired of being the victim of hypocrisy by a set of people who supposedly practice democracy and the Gandhian non-violence. We are the victims of violence. Nowhere, and at no time, the upper caste/ Hindus became victims of our violence. Then how can they charge me with being blood-thirsty? Who conducted these anti-reservation wars and violence against the Mandal Commission Report in Sept-Oct.1990 all over India? In the 1984 "Blue Star Operation" and the anti-Sikh riots, in the 1992 Babri Masjid demolition and in the 2002 Gujarat Genocide?

Our fight is for our human rights. We want freedom — liberation by any means necessary. We want justice by any means necessary. We want equality by any means necessary. That is all. We want our share. We want proportional representation. We don't want to steal the upper caste share. They should be entitled to their share. Even if they want a "*savarna* homeland", we are prepared to concede that. They will have their share. And we will have ours: in proportion to the population of each section. Is this not a fair demand?

What Malcolm X said

This is what that great Black American leader, Malcolm X, said:

> "A man with a rifle or a club can only be stopped by a person who defends himself with a rifle or a club. That's equality. If you have a dog, I must have a dog. If you have a rifle, I must have a rifle. This is equality. If the United States Government doesn't want you and me to get rifles, then take the rifles away from those racists. If they don't want you and me to use clubs, take the clubs away from the racists. If they don't want you and me to get violent, then stop the racists from being violent. Don't teach us non-violence while those cracks are violent. Those days are over."

This is what Malcolm X said.

You cannot arm only the upper castes (Hindus). They have the police, military. They have the media. The courts. The mighty govt. is also on their side. But we have none. So we should be the first to be armed.

Self-Protection

Q: They say arming Dalits will lead to more violence. The moral fibre of the country will be broken.

A: Tactics based solely on morality can succeed only when we are dealing with a people who are moral or a system that is moral. A man or system which oppresses another man because of his *jati*, birth, colour, gender is not moral. It is the duty of every SC/ST/BC and Muslim/Christian/Sikh throughout this country to protect their people against upper caste violence of all varieties.

Gandhi & "*Harijan*" welfare

Q: Gandhi is famous for "*Harijan* welfare" and his whole life was devoted for the Untouchables. What do you say?

A: The upper caste rulers are so deceptive that they change their names, colour, idiom, style but never their exploitation. This is my experience. M.K. Gandhi was the latest and the most famous trickster. He called us by a new name, *Harijan*, but he did not change our condition or our slavery. The rulers only change the tricks. This is done from Delhi right down to the village level.

That is why Babasaheb Ambedkar called Gandhi the Enemy No.1 of Untouchables. And we have any number of Gandhis even today.

We need allies

Q: Are you satisfied with your strategy and tactics to fight the oppressors?

A: A philosophy is different. Strategy and tactics are different. Karl Marx wrote only the philosophy. But Lenin implemented marxism through his strategies and tactics. That means if Lenin had not been born not only marxism would have been unheard of but even Karl Marx would have been unknown. So strategies and tactics are equally important if not more important than philosophy itself.

Since our Brahminical rulers are past masters in tricks (their strategies and tactics), we have to resort to superior strategies and tactics to defeat their designs. We have got to seek some new methods, a reappraisal of the situation, some new methods for attacking it or solving it and a new direction and new allies.

Read my book, *Weapons to Fight Counter Revolution*, (DSA–2004, Rs. 75) in which I have perfected ten deadliest weapons.

Gandhian *satyagraha*

We actually need allies who are going to help us achieve a victory, not allies who are going to tell us to be non–violent. We had enough of such *mahatmas* who tell us that if one is hit on one cheek, he must turn the other cheek. We want allies who will tell us that if we are hit on one cheek, we will cut the very neck of the enemy. Tooth for tooth. Eye for an eye. Non–violent with those who are non–violent. But violence with the bully.

Q: Do you agree with protests like hunger strike, *satyagraha*, pen-down strike, slogan-shouting, wall-writing, pamphleteering and such other popular "democratic" form of protests?

A: The days of demonstrations or protests are over. They are outdated. All that does is to put you in the jail. Stop this business of *satyagraha*, hunger strike. Why should we starve? Why should we go hungry? Our people have starved enough. Now is the time for us to eat well and always eat well (don't over-eat). I am fed up with these gandhian gimmicks. These are the weapons of the weak.

Always offensive, not defensive

A protest demonstration, a *jatha*, *morcha*, a procession is an act that is a reaction to someone else's action. Don't allow yourself to be put on the defensive. We will win only if we are constantly on the offensive. Don't allow the enemy to put you on the defensive. Be constantly on the offensive. Put the enemy on the defensive.

A demonstration is alright if it is going to get results. But rarely it does. Fed up with these parsimonious humbug. All these "democratic" way of protests are prescribed to us by our oppressors. Because they want us to fail. They can use police, military and everything else to inflict violence on us. While being violent they are advising us to be non-violent. Nonsense. Don't listen to these cheats. Non-violence is the language of the coward. In India, nobody has succeeded through non-violence. Even Gandhi used only violence against the British but always calling it non-violence.

Internationalising Dalit problem

Q: Why do you want to internationalise the Dalit problem? Why wash our dirty linen in public ?

A: We have to make the world see that the problem that we are confronted with is a problem of entire humanity. That we are fighting against man's inhumanity to man. It is not merely an economic problem. It's not merely an Indian problem. It is not merely a racial problem. It is a mental problem. And this mentally sick people are spreading their sickness to the whole world. So, you and I have to warn the world that if it is not nipped in the bud this contagious disease will spread all over the world. We have to make the world aware that there will be no peace on this earth as long as our (Dalit) human rights are being violated in India.

Nay. It is the world's biggest problem because the Aryan racism has caused two World Wars and if not checked, it may cause the more deadly Third World War which may destroy the whole world. (Read: *Brahminism*, DSA-2002).

You must accept this. If you are not for that, you are not for freedom. It means you don't even want to be a human being. You don't want to pay the price that is necessary. And you should not even be allowed around us, other humans, if you don't want to pay the price. Those who have the commitment will have to pay for it, suffer for it, die for it.

Antagonising upper castes

Q: You say the future belongs to Dalits. Then why should Dalits be impatient to fight and antagonise the upper castes? Anyway, the upper castes are losing.

A: There are so many of us who think that since the future belongs to us "let me relax for the present". This attitude is helping the Enemy. We relax but the Enemy doesn't. They are ever vigilant, because being the property-holders, it is they who stand to lose. They are looking in all directions, watching for the assault. But our people are sleeping. We call this "slaves enjoying their slavery". It is true that the future belongs to us. That doesn't mean we can rest. Eternal vigilance is the price of democracy.

You must know that ever since the Brahmins defeated Budhism 2,500 years ago, they have not met with any single defeat. Defeating this deadly enemy is no joke.

The art of dying

Q: You say Dalits must not rest. They must fight and fight. But in the course of fight if they die, is this not a setback to your movement?

A: The price is death, really. The price to make others respect your human rights is death. You have to be ready to die or else you have to be ready to take the life of the oppressor. Liberty or death. Life, liberty, the pursuit of happiness. Or else kill me. Treat me like a man, or kill me. This is what you have to say.

Those who want to live must first know how to die. Only those who know how to die will know how to live.

Palestinians, particularly the Hamas, have taught this to the whole world. Suicide bombing is not violence. This is intelligence. As soon as you start merely thinking like that, they say you are advocating violence. But we never advocate violence. We are advocating intelligence.

The suicide bomber dies first before the others die. So, how it can be dubbed terrorism? It is supreme sacrifice.

We want peace

We are peace-mongers. Not war-mongers. We always want peace. All producers of wealth, all over the world, need peace. But all destroyers of wealth need war and violence. They are always violent. We are the producers of wealth and hence advocates of peace. It is the destroyers of wealth who call us violent.

It's time for you and me now to let the world know how peaceful we are, how well-meaning we are, how law-abiding we are. But at the same time, we have to let the same world know we will blow their world sky-high if we are not respected, recognised and treated like other human beings. For this we must first know how to die.

There is no point in living the life of a cockroach. We must live as a human being. When we are not allowed to live as human beings, let us sacrifice ourselves, die for the sake of our children, our grandchildren so that they may live as human beings. This is what we call the art of living.

Only those who have mastered the art of dying can know the art of living.

Dalit problem is a world problem

Q: How to master this art of dying?

A: One of the first steps toward our being able to do

this is to internationalise our problem. Untouchables together with the Tribals form a third of India's 1,000-odd million population. So we form the single largest "persecuted minority" in the world. So, automatically our problem becomes a world problem. We must make the world know that our problem is their problem. It's a problem for the entire humanity.

India cannot be free until all Dalits are free. We form a third of Indian population and inhabit every village of India.

Ballot and bullet

Q: Freedom to India, you say, did not help your people, so how to get freedom to your people?

A: We have wasted a lot of our time begging, protesting, petitioning, complaining. This "peaceful" protests have taken us nowhere. This gandhian humbug will not take us anywhere.

Only two things will bring us freedom — ballot or bullet. Only two things. Well, if you and I use the ballot and still don't get freedom, we're going to be forced to use the bullet.

We have 125 Dalit MPs in Parliament. What have they achieved? Our slave-masters tell us to stick to ballot. But ballot is successful only in an equal society. In an unequal society, ballot is a waste.

So, the only way we can get them to change their laws is by becoming involved with the ballot. This also we are trying. We have the best of legislations for our protection. But these laws are not enforced because those in charge of law-enforcement are the very slave-masters. So it is proved that the ballot won't do. There is no other alternative but the bullet. Liberty or death. That means the ballot or the bullet. I only pray that we will not be forced to take to bullets.

Violent words

Q: Your sincerity is not doubted but the way you put forward your argument is not polite, decent. Why are you violent even in words? Polemics spoil your case.

A: History of this country has proved that "polite" people have never been successful in bringing about any kind of advantages to the Dalits. Do-gooders. The bum-lickers. The *chamchas* of the Hindus are the real danger. You have to walk in with a hand grenade and tell the man: "Listen, you give us what we want, our human rights, or else you are in danger". Then only he will listen to you. But if you go in there polite and acting responsible and sane, you are wasting your time. You have to be insane with insane people. You have to be cunning with crooked people.

For saying this, will I be charged with advocating violence? Let me show you what a rotten system this is. They say I am advocating violence. But they don't say that Bal Thackeray is advocating violence. They won't say that the Hindu terrorist party of RSS is preaching violence. They won't say that the *Ramayana* and *Mahabharata* are inciting violence. If the ruling class tries to use violence against us, it is described as "tackling law and order". But when we protest against suppression of our human rights, we are dubbed hate-teachers.

Human rights of Brahmins

I want to restate my case clearly. I believe in human rights for every one, including the Brahmins. None of us is qualified to judge each other. Neither I should have that authority. Nor you. We should not have the right to force anyone to walk with us. Nor do we have the right to condemn those who want to be separate. If my brother or son wants to leave me and wants to have a separate house, he has all the right. What we say is we are all equals. But at the same time separate. Equal but separate. Not high or low.

The principle is you can't put your hand into my pocket, and I can't put into yours. They can't say that you are "meritless". You are an idiot. And hence unfit to rule. Even the meritless, even the idiot has the right to rule and exist. All racist societies say that "merit" is their monopoly. And only meritocrats must rule. But the slaves say: To hell with your merit. Self-govt. is any day better than an efficient govt. (Read my book, *Merit—My Foot*, DSA-2006).

Dog eating dog

Q: There is lot of division and disunity among Dalits. Can't you unite them?

A: No. That is not our job. Unity comes out of crisis. When there is no crisis, Dalits are disunited. There is nothing wrong with division or disunity. If some of our Dalit brothers want to establish a separate organisation, that is their right. We must learn to wish them well and mean it. Our fight must never be against each other. Dog does not eat dog. Some brothers broke away from Kanshi Ram and called their BAMCEF as the genuine one. That is perfectly alright. But we must not quarrel with each other. No matter how much we differ over minor things, our fight must be directed always against the common enemy.

Remember, dog doesn't eat dog. Even the dog has that much of sense. But some of us are worse than the dog. Wherever you go and whatever you do, remember that we are all still brothers and sisters and we all still share the same problem.

You may be a Jagjivan Ram, a *crorepati*, a Deputy Prime Minister. But Hindus hate you. You may be a big, powerful officer. You may be anything. Still you are an Untouchable.

Let us, therefore, not waste time condemning and fighting each other. We have already wasted too much time and energy doing this in the past.

There is enough scope for fishing. The Arabian sea coast is so vast. You fish in one corner. And another can fish in another corner. But you can't say that you alone shall fish and others have no right to fish. The Brahminical forces divide us only through this way.

On non-violence

Q: Please elaborate your case on non-violence?

A: Non-violence is being advertised by our violent oppressors to prevent us from taking to armed struggle. Non-violence is only for us. But they can be violent to any extent.

Non-violence has become outdated. It only helps the

Enemy. But at the same time the Enemy knows that once 1/3 of India's people (Dalits) stop being confined to a non-violent approach by joining hands with their co-sufferers (Muslims/Sikhs/Christians) and fight back the minuscule ruling class, you're going to have a different situation. The real genuine non-violence will come into operation only after the Dalits take over the country.

Hinduism, the religion of our upper caste oppressors, is the world's most violent religion. They and their leader, M.K. Gandhi, are preaching non-violence to us so that we don't become violent.

Stooges among Dalits

Q: What are the tricks used by the rulers to enslave Dalits?

A: The rulers use new and newer tricks. They frantically search for the best stooge among Dalits and confer their glorious Peace Prize for being non-violent, and shout that it lent strength to the non-violent movement. See what they did with Mandela. Non-violence is a trick that is forced on our people to keep us away from even being able to defend ourselves. Mohandas Karamchand Gandhi used this non-violent weapon to inflict the worst violence against us. If the South African Blacks are the victims of violence, we are the victims of non-violence in India.

Our upper caste oppressors are always on the look out for stooges among us, confer on them all sorts of awards and rewards like "Alternate Nobel Prize", "Magsasay Award" etc. etc. and parade them under a floodlight of publicity to silence and overawe the revolutionaries among us. These stooges raise lot of dust during their lifetime but do not raise the level of our people even by an inch. Beware of such stooges of Brahminical people.

The language of cowards

Most Hindu leaders who profess to support Dalit struggle are usually with us as long as our people are "non-violent". And they are the ones who encourage them to be non-violent. That means they want us to "love" our oppressors. They ask you to turn the other cheek. But those who are genuinely for the freedom of the Black Untouchables cannot be advocates of non-violence. Did I not say that non-violence is the language of the cowards. Violence for self-defence is no violence. If you don't defend yourself, the advocate of non-violence will kill you. So violence for self-defence has to be used wherever necessary. Remember: Self-defence has the support of law and also all religions.

In Islam, they call it *jehad* (struggle). The struggle of the oppressed to defend themselves has the religious sanction.

You can even kill in self-defence. This is perfectly legal. Don't run away. Don't go to the police station to complain. You won't get justice there. Don't behave like cowards. Kill before the killer kills you.

On religion

Q: What are your views on religion?

A: A person's choice of religion is her or his personal affair. But I must say that Brahminism was inflicted on us, on our people, not to take us to heaven but to make us good slaves, primarily by robbing us of our human rights to defend ourselves in the name of Rama and Krishna — the two mischievous Aryan gods who have played the worst havoc on our lives. Our leader, our saviour, our liberator, Dr. Babasaheb Ambedkar, had told us that we are not Hindu and were never Hindu. We were only made "Hindu" for the benefit of the upper castes. In the cow-belt, almost every Dalit invariably has either Ram in the beginning or the end of his name. Jagjivan Ram, Ram Dhan, Kanshi Ram. Who is this Ram (Read Dr. B.R. Ambedkar's book, *Riddles of Rama & Krishna*, DSA-1995, Rs. 10). Our people must stop keeping these two names and thus disown these two gods and their religion of slavery. In the cow-belt our people are told to greet each other as "Ram-Ram". But upper castes say *namaste*. They have effectively used these two gods to enslave us. This must stop. Say *Jai Bhim*. That is the revolutionary way of greeting. Don't say *Jai Hind*.

God & religion

Q: Should the Dalits believe in god and religion?

A: Which god? This is a funny question. The original inhabitants of India, that is the SC/ST/BCs, are all pre-Aryan. They had their own deities. They had their own rich religions. Their own simple customs and manners. Even today in all the villages of India these three sections are following their own religions and worshipping their own deities. The only difference between the religions of these peoples and the religions of Hinduism, Islam, Christianity etc. is that the latter are "organised religions" and the religions of the former are not. Nevertheless, they are religions. The pre-Aryan peoples even today are matriarchal. Women enjoy supremacy. The Aryan society is male-dominated and anti-woman. SC/ST/BC deities are mostly female. And meat--eaters. They drink and eat meat. But non-violent. The Aryan gods are vegetarian but violent.

So, the SC/ST/BCs in rural areas believe even today in their own ancient religions and their powerful deities and offer them chicken, pig and liquor and then consume it. The pre-Aryan SC/ST/BCs have nothing to do with the Aryan religion (Hinduism) or their gods or scriptures. They should not worship Hindu gods, go to their temples, observe Hindu festivals or keep Hindu names. Not that we have anything against them. When we have such a glorious cultural heritage of the Indus Valley Civilisation which is ours, why shine in a borrowed garment and lose our **identity**?

There is nothing wrong in believing in god or religion. We are not against anybody's god or religion. We are not even against Brahminical gods or their religion. Since many of our gods have been "stolen" by the Brahminical Social Order to make it appear as the "Hindu majority religion" and fitted into their caste system as "upper" or "lower castes", our people have started losing their **identity**.

After having suffered suffocation under the Brahminical gas chamber, many of them realised their mistakes and escaped into the more egalitarian religions and got converted to Islam, Christianity, Sikhism, Budhism. The 25% so-called "religious minorities" of India are mostly converts from SC/ST/BCs.

Religious conversion

Q: Do you support religious conversion?

A: Yes. Conversion has done lot of good to our people. Those Dalits in East Bengal (Bangladesh) got an independent country of their own because they got converted to Islam. Those who embraced Sikhism got the right to bear arms. Conversion brought them identity, dignity. So we are all for conversion. (Dr. B.R. Ambedkar, *Why Go for Conversion?* DSA-1987).

To protect these hapless chicken from the rampaging hawks (organised religions), Babasaheb Ambedkar asked our people to embrace Budhism which was the religion of the entire pre-Aryan India before it was destroyed by Brahminism. There is an urgent need for an organised massive conversion drive towards Budhism as outlined in Babasaheb's book, *Buddha & His Dhamma.* Once our people quit Hinduism and embrace Budhism they will get back their **identity** and along with that their human rights (reservations).

Ends & means

Q: Gandhi made much of "means" and "ends", saying means justify the end. What do you say?

A: Babasaheb Ambedkar has given us the political, economic and social solution to all our complicated problems. He has shown us the path and none to this day has bettered it. But I am one of those who is willing to try any means necessary to bring an end to the injustices our people suffer. It is not possible to prescribe one solution to the ills of the country as a whole because our people are also divided by language, territory and ethnic identity. They also are from different social background. We cannot have one common solution to the problems of all Dalits and Adivasis. So we can adopt any means suiting to the genius of that area.

Will Dalits rule India ?

I can clearly foresee the day when the Black Dalit culture will be the dominant culture of India and when the Black Dalit will be the dominant person. When I say Black person will be the "dominant person", I don't mean the Blacks will dominate the rest. People who have been dominated for centuries will not dominate others. What I mean is that, the Black (Dalit) culture will be the future culture. Not only in India but of the whole world. So far, the Black was made to look ugly, uncouth, despised, meritless, brainless, stinking, idiotic. But the Black is now poised to become beautiful. Already its rumblings are heard. Black is beautiful.

Q: You say that the Brahminical forces are *hinduising* (enslaving) the Dalits and Adivasis; so much so when the Dalits take over will not this be a Brahminical Dalit rule?

Caste identity

A: This question is often put to me. Is there a danger in India that the Untouchables will get diluted and dissolved in the Hindu culture? Will the Hindus succeed in "assimilating" the Dalits? I say no. Several centuries of their efforts have not succeeded. What was not possible so far in the past 2,500 years cannot be made possible now. Dalits will never, ever have "integration" with Hindus. Right now, the two are like the snake and the mongoose.

Dalits are Untouchables. It means they are untouched by the Hindu contamination. They are "outcastes" meaning outside the caste system. They have nothing to do with Hindu or their Hinduism. We belong to a separate religion, a great pre-Aryan religion. "Integration" would destroy our people. Babasaheb Ambedkar has said Untouchables are not Hindu and were never Hindu. They could not *hinduise* us in the past thousands of years. How could they succeed now?

No doubt the Hindus are trying their best to *hinduise* (enslave) us. The entire current unrest, violence is arising out of our resistance to their *hinduisation* exercise. But no SC/ST/BC *jati* has lost its **identity**. Please read our book, *Caste — A Nation Within the Nation* (Books for Change, 2002).

Dog defending its master

Q: Despite so much of violence, why the Dalits are not hitting back at their oppressors? Why there is no Dalit uprising in any part of India?

A: It is true that the Brahminical Social Order has reduced us to the level of a dog. The dog is a ferocious animal. But no matter how ferocious the dog is, you shout at the dog on the street and it will run away putting its tail under its buttock. Its master has never trained it how to defend itself. You throw a stone at the dog inside its master's compound, you had it. It will pounce on you. You see the difference. You throw a stone outside its master's compound. It will simply sulk and run away. But if you walk through the master's gate, the same dog will growl and bite. Why will it growl and bite over there and not growl and bite over outside? It is growling and biting for the defence of its master and the benefit of its master. But when its own interests are threatened it has no growl, no anger. Funny. Is it not? This is our problem.

Why should we die for others?

Our people have become exactly like that dog. We have become like that bulldog defending its master — but not itself. Many of us in India have died defending the upper castes, our oppressors. We are the most violent soldiers that India has when it comes to defending the upper castes. But when our mothers and our own property are being attacked, we are "non-violent". We simply don't get angry. This must stop. Enough of our people have died in defence of upper castes. We acted as their foot soldiers to kill Muslims and Sikhs. They used the Backward Castes to attack Dalits. But are the Muslims, Sikhs, BCs our enemies? No. They are our own people, yet we killed them at the behest of our upper caste masters. This must stop.

Look at the Palestinians and their heroic fighting arm, Hamas. They have been fighting the zionist aggressors for 100 years or so. Palestine has become the world's longest lasting humanitarian problem in which thousands and thousands of Palestinians (Arabs) died. Yet they have not given up. They are dying in hundreds. The Jews having property are not willing to die. Those who are not ready to die will not know how to die.

We must stop dying for others and must start dying for ourselves. I call this the art of dying. We must cultivate the art of dying - dying to defend our own people.

Dalit heroes

Q: Hindus have so many heroes and heroines. Do you have any?

A: When we select heroines and heroes, about which our children ought to be taught, we must select Dalit heroines and heroes who have died fighting for the benefit of our own people. We have never taught them about Ayyankali, Mahatma Phule, Sant Ravidas, Dr. B.R. Ambedkar, Periyar E.V. Ramaswamy, Dr. Lohia, Tipu Sultan and hundreds of others. This is the kind of history we are taught. Because in India those who make history are different. Those who write history are different.

Phoolan Devi, the greatest Dalit heroine

Our oppressors are telling us that Phoolan Devi was a dacoit. What the hell they mean by that? Long back I had suggested to put her up to the Assembly elections even as she was rotting in the Gwalior jail. But Kanshi Ram told me that since her name was not in the voters list, she could not be put up as a candidate. I can tell you Phoolan Devi is the greatest Dalit woman who fought for the human rights of Dalit women. She killed only those Thakurs who were responsible for her rape.

Stop calling us naxalites

Q: We hear so many naxalite groups (Marxist-Leninist-Maoists) taking to armed struggle. But why your people have not taken up arms?

A: Our oppressors are calling Dalits and Adivasis fighting for our human rights as naxalites. This is nonsense. How can people fighting for human rights be dubbed naxalites? This is just to defame our people. These innocent tribals are fighting for their human rights and to save the honour of their women. The criminals are the upper castes. But the upper caste press and the upper caste police describe these human rights fighters as "naxalites" so that they could be dubbed violent and put behind the bars. These so-called naxalites know nothing of naxalism or naxalites. They are pure and simple tribal people. India's Marxist-Leninist-Maoist parties controlled by the upper castes (Hindus) are committing a crime by describing our people as naxalites so that they may be nabbed and handed over to police. Naxalism, therefore, is an upper caste conspiracy to enslave our people.

The upper castes of India, forming less than 15% of our population, have neither learnt anything new nor forgotten anything old. They are also badly divided. Vertically and also horizontally. Each *jati* is trying to cut the other *jati*'s throat. Even within the *jati* there is so much of jealousy and ill-feeling.

Unity of upper castes

But in fighting us they (upper castes) are all one. They have the media to defame us. They have the gods to curse us. They have the money to manipulate us. They call our people naxalites. They call us anti-national. They say we are "terrorists". They say we are "secessionists". All sorts of names are used to defame and demoralise our people. They say we are foreign-funded. They say we are "extremists". They say we are divisionists. There is no word of abuse which they have not used against us. But we have survived all these character assassinations because we are pure Untouchables and Adivasis (Tribals).

Uprooting Brahminical values

Our enemies say we are fanatics, subversives, seditious. But nowhere you can get a more law-abiding person than a Dalit.

It is a fact that today we are living in an era of revolution — which means an era of change — when people who are being oppressed want a change. Yes, we want change. Not mere change: transformation. We don't want that change that comes year by year, or week by week, or month by month. We can't endlessly wait. We want a change here and now — a complete uprooting of the Brahminical values.

When a person places a proper value on freedom, there is nothing under the sun that he will not do to acquire that freedom. A person who believes in freedom will do anything under the sun to acquire or achieve this freedom and she or he will do anything under the sun to preserve that freedom. To us our human rights are the most important. We can do anything to get our human rights restored.

We prefer non-violence. But if you are violent, we will be doubly violent. Violence is unavoidable. Any price is good enough to get our lost rights. Our oppressors must note that they cannot object to our people dying for their lost rights. As long as we don't cultivate the art of dying, we cannot cultivate the art of living. Remember the suicide bomber. We need such people ready for such supreme sacrifice.

Role of youth

Q: Do you have full faith in the youth?

A: No. Not all youth. No doubt the youth and students in particular all over the world are the ones who bring about a change. Old people don't want change because iron has entered into their soul. I am not criticising old people. There are also some old people with young mind. If you are ready for some action you are not old. And there are some young people with old mind. I don't care how old you are. But if you are not ready for some action, I don't care how young you are, you are old. As long as you want some action, you are young. But any time you begin to sit on the fence, compromising with the enemy and your toes start shaking because you are afraid of too much action, then you are too old. You are a shirker. Such people must get out of the way. Some people look too old even in their youth. Brahminical racist values have made us cowards. We have stopped thinking because we have kept our brains in the deep-freezer of a Sharma or a Dwivedi and our brains got rusted too much.

Dalits alone should represent Dalits

Q: Will you allow a Brahmin to represent the Dalits?

A: A Brahmin can never represent the Dalits. We should never let him represent us. That doesn't mean we hate them. We hate no individual. We hate only the system. When we say that a Hindu can't represent us what we mean is we simply don't trust them. We have nothing against them. Snakes are known to bite us and poison us. The result is death. So we avoid snakes. That doesn't mean we hate the snake. We don't trust the snake even if it comes to us and begs us that it will be our friend. Because we know it is a poisonous creature. Like that snake, we don't trust the upper castes. That's all.

The Brahmins have started all sorts of *natak* (drama) companies to fool our people. The Medha Patkars, the Agniveshas etc. are killing our revolutionary spirit. Why should our people be led by Brahmins? Our own people should lead. Reject outside leadership.

It is our job today to represent ourselves just as the upper castes are representing themselves. We don't need someone else representing us. We don't want anybody to tell us how we should think. We will directly deal with the world and make it know how we think. We don't want a Brahmin spokesman to tell the world how we think. We want the world to know how we think. We also want the world to know that we don't like what the upper castes are doing for us inside India. We have to be blunt.

Sweet talk produces no fire

We have to be always cut and dry. No mercy on the exploiters. And if you can't talk that tough language, he doesn't even hear you. He understands only the blunt language — that hit-to-kill language. You can come talking that old sweet talk, or that old peace talk, or that old non-violent talk. The upper caste man doesn't hear that kind of talk. He will pat you on your back and tell that you are a good guy and give you a Peace Prize. Why they gave it to Mother Theresa? And Mandela? Why they didn't give a Nobel Peace prize to

Babasaheb? Because Babasaheb waged a war on Hindus. And Malcolm X fought the Whites. He never listened to their peace music. I did not get any award. But Hindus gave me lots of rewards— jail, dismissal, passport impounded. Anybody getting an award or reward from Hindus is a suspect in our eyes.

Courage is not for sale

How can we get a Peace Prize when the war is not yet over? I am all for peace, but the only way I can preserve peace is by being prepared for war. Talk peace but keep the powder dry. Keeping finger on the trigger, only then we must talk peace. But if you talk peace, you are certain to have the war. Non-violence is the language of the cowards. M.K. Gandhi preached non-violence for us, but not to the upper caste hounds.

Q: Do you think the time has come to fight the upper castes? They are powerful not merely physically but their Brahminical ideology governs and controls also the Dalits?

A: Yes, you are right. But that doesn't mean we should keep quiet. Never say that the odds are against us. I don't even want to hear that. Those who think the odds are against us, please forget the very thought of it. The odds are not against you. The odds are against you only when you are scared. Cowards alone speak like that. The only thing that makes you think that odds are against you is cowardice. Get rid of that fear and launch the struggle.

Q: But how to get courage?

A: I know what you mean. Courage or fear is a state of mind. You can't buy "courage" in a shop. You can't go to a shop and ask for a rupee worth of courage. Courage is not for sale. I can't steel your courage. I can't make you courageous. Courage comes from within. Courage comes out of conviction. All people with conviction and commitment will be courageous. You are your own architect. You have to cultivate the art of being courageous. But the Brahminical society has made us hate ourselves. Self-hatred infused inferiority complex in us and we became cowards. So we must decide to shed fear. This is very easy.

How to fight the enemy?

We must get rid of that fright in our hearts. There is no such thing as odds against you. Because when that blackguard knows that when he starts playing with you, his intention is to persecute you. But if he comes to know that when he is playing with you, you are going to hit back, he will be cut to size. We must be peaceful, respectable and responsible only with peaceful, respectable and responsible people. Eye for an eye. Tooth for a tooth. Shoot him down before he kills you. The Indian Penal Code and the Criminal Procedure Code sanction murder in self-defence.

Let him know that you are peaceful. Let him know that you are respectful. Let him know that you respect him. Let him know that you are law-abiding. Let him know that you want to be a good citizen. Let him know that all those right-thinking things. But let him also know that at the same time that you are ready to do to him what he has been trying to do to you. Then only you will always have peace. I assure, you will always have it. Learn a lesson from history.

Peace or justice?

Q: Don't you think that if the Dalits take to violence the country will have no peace? And more so, the country's unity and integrity will be broken to pieces?

A: This is a typical upper caste argument. We are fed up with this one-way peace. Dr. Babasaheb Ambedkar, made our Constitution though he was not happy with it. Still we have no intention to break the Constitution. We want peace. But peace can't be imposed at the cost of justice. If justice is broken, we will break the peace. Remember, peace is never at the cost of justice. What peace? Who wants this peace of the graveyard?

Can Dalits destroy Brahminism?

Q: Everybody has failed to destroy Brahminism? Can Dalits do it?

A: Don't go by their game. Don't play the game by their rules. Let them know now that this is a new game, and we have got some new rules. And these rules mean anything that is Brahminical is poison to us. Between a person with a Brahminical ideology and a human being we choose to be the latter. A Brahminical person cannot be a human being. Their "sacred scriptures", their gods, their graded society have emasculated us. We have to level them down with the new rules. And remember, only we can do it. None else. Remember, even those living in the Brahminical Social Order are not happy with

Brahminism. Only we can make them happy.

Are you listening, sisters and brothers? I know you are with me. This is an anguished call. Our country has stopped growing. It is decaying. The Brahminical Social Order has killed our youth, destroyed their talents. Half the country's population comprising its women, are imprisoned in the kitchen. All these people have to be liberated. Only we can do it.

Q: They say you are casteist, communal.

A: The Brahminical press has purposely and skillfully projected me in the image of a casteist, communalist and anti-communist - both sectarian, a divider, a Brahmin-baiter, an extremist, terrorist, anti-national. And what not. But I don't care. I treat these toilet papers with the contempt it deserves.

Dalit nationalism

Q: How do you define Dalit nationalism which you have been so vociferously advocating?

A: I define Dalit nationalism as the idea that the Dalits should control the socio-economic steering wheel of the community, the politics of this community and so forth. The Hindus cannot govern us. Nor do we intend to control the Hindus.

We demand self-determination even for Brahmins. Proportional representation for everybody. You can't put your hand into my pocket. Nor I can put mine into yours. Self-determination to each unit however small it is. Each caste, or even subcaste must gets its share.

On violence & non-violence

Q: Coming back to the subject, is it true that you favour violence?

A: I am fed up of answering this question. I don't favour violence. How can the very victims of violence favour violence? If we can bring about recognition and respect to our people by peaceful means, well and good. Everybody would like to reach her or his objectives peacefully. But I must also be a realist.

Why only we in this country are asked to be non-violent? Why this question is directed only at Muslims, Sikhs and Tribals? I have never heard anybody going to the Rashtriya Swayamsevak Sangh (RSS) or the Shiv Sena and such terrorist outfits and teaching them non-violence. Why none asked this question to the killer of M.K. Gandhi? Non-violence is preached only to non-Hindu indigenous Indians. And I don't like anyone teaching non-violence only to our people until someone at the same time is teaching our oppressors to be non-violent. I repeat the words of Malcom X: "We should protect ourselves by any means necessary when we are attacked by racists".

Corrupt education system

Q: Racism or caste hatred instead of coming down is actually increasing in India. Has it got anything to do with our education system?

A: Yes. Our entire education system is Brahminical, anti-social and hence corrupt. If the entire Indian population had been properly educated — I mean given a true picture of the history and contributions of the Dalits — I think many upper castes would have been less racist in their feelings. Our textbooks, our toilet papers, TV and Radio are injecting racism daily. The entire thing should be shot down and new humanist education system has to take over.

Rewriting history

Q: Do you advocate re-writing of our history books?

A: Brahminical writers have distorted our history. It is but natural that those who want to control the present do it by controlling the past. The Hindu terrorist claim on the Babri Masjid is a good example of this fabrication of history. But such mischief-mongers do not know that they may temporarily control the present. But by so doing they will damage the future of the society. This is what the Brahminical forces are doing by distorting the history of India. So, we the Dalit people want the entire history of India to be written as history should be written. And since we can't trust the upper castes to do this, we call upon the Dalit historians to do it with the support of international historians with the aid of the UN and UNESCO.

Set fire to education system

Had there been a correct, truthful history, the upper castes would have become more human and shown more respect for the Dalits as human beings. Knowing about the Dalit contributions to science and civilisation in the past, this Aryan feelings of false superiority would have been at least partially negated. Also, this feeling of inferiority that the Dalits suffer from would be replaced by a balanced knowledge of himself. He would feel more like a human being. He would function more like a human being in a society of human beings. He would stop hating himself, his name, his parents, his food, his people. So, history is the key. I call upon Dalits to address themselves to repairing the Indian history. (V.T Rajshekar, *Aggression on Indian Culture*, DSA-2001, & *Grave-Diggers of History*, DSA-2001).

So, a good education is necessary to eliminate all the prejudices. And just because we have colleges, universities, doesn't mean we have a good education. Our colleges and universities, don't give good education. Our colleges and universities in the Indian educational system are skillfully used to mis-educate, misinterpret and brainwash our people in Brahminical value system. We must set fire to the existing education system. And replace it with a humanist, scientific system. When the country was less educated, we did not have so much problems. More education led to more problems. It is the highly educated Hindu who is a rabid racist. Look at our IITs and IIMs. They are the hot beds of Hindu nazism. Most poisonous snakes are produced in our centres of higher learning. We have to bombard them.

That is why I say no education is better than bad education. India's countryside, where uneducated, innocents live, see no anti-Muslim or anti-Christian riots. Hindu terrorists use cities as their battle ground because city is the abode of the "educated".

Q: Can you give a concrete example of falsifying history?

A: Untouchables, tribals and Backward Castes are all pre-Aryan tribes. Hinduism or Brahminism/*vaidik dharma/ sanathan dharma* was brought to India by the invading

Aryan barbarians. After coming to India, they tried to play with our people. But our people fought back. Never did our people compromise with the Aryans. But since about 200 years or so — only about 200 years — they have been injecting their Hindu poison into our people—changing their name, capturing our shrines and adopting our deities. And making many of our "educated" people think that they belong to the *shudra varna.* All this is false. Our people are not Hindu and have nothing to do with Hindu. Hence the urgent need to re-write our history.

Incitement to violence

Q: Your writings are inciting Dalits to violence. Why can't you change your style?

A: Why do you go on repeating this upper caste charge? There is no proof for it. No court has convicted me so far for incitement. In fact, the violence that exists in India today is the violence of which the Dalits are the victims. I have never advocated our people going out and initiating any acts of aggression against upper castes. You show me one proof of my advocating violence, either in my writings or speeches.

In defence of polemics

But the govt. documents themselves have hundreds of evidences of the Dalit being a continual victim of the violent actions committed by the upper caste nazi elements. If the Indian govt. has shown itself unwilling or unable to protect us, our lives and our property, the honour of our women that itself is the proof of the upper caste violence against us. Our failure to retaliate is non–

violence. That only proves that Dalits are the most non-violent people of India. But who is there to write this? We have no media.

Our leader, Babasaheb Ambedkar, has given his famous "Three Commandments" and said that this is the time for our people to "Educate, Agitate and Organise" and unitedly protect ourselves, to defend ourselves against this violence. Now, if this amounts to advocating violence, then I am shocked at the lack of proper understanding on the part of the rulers. Victims of violence dubbed violent? Ever heard of it anywhere?

For details please read our signed article in the *Dalit Voice* May 16, 2006 p.24: "*In defence of polemics*".

Charge of casteism

Q: Instead of taking up casteist postures, why don't you advocate the cause of all the poor people irrespective of caste or religion?

A: This is another stupid charge against me. There are people accusing me of being a casteist. But I am not a casteist in any way. My whole life, my family is an example of this. I oppose and fight caste system in all its form, shape, size, colour and name. I have taken an uncompromising stand against all forms of untouchability, racism and discrimination that are based on caste, colour, creed, religion and race.

I myself do not judge a person by the colour of his skin or his birth. The yardstick that I use to judge a person is her or his deeds, behaviour, intentions — rather the ethical content. Your heart - not the head. The value system.

Poverty based struggle

But the Brahminical media has very skillfully projected me in the image of a casteist simply because I take an uncompromising stand against the caste system that is the bedrock of Hinduism. The very victim of caste system is called a casteist. Heard of it anywhere? What kind of a logic is this? Caste is a Hindu institution. Hindus are boiling in the hot waters of caste system. They too have to be saved. But the SC/ST/BCs are casteless outcastes being non-Hindus. What is called "caste" among SC/ST/BCs is their ethnic identity. I am not for destruction of these ethnic identities. India is a multinational country. And every identity must be preserved. Rather it must be strengthened. (V.T. Rajshekar, *Caste- A Nation Within the Nation*, Books for Change, 2002).

I think it is an injustice, not only to me but to the whole country that is being misled in this way by the casteist media, especially at a time when efforts are being made by well-meaning people to bring the various social segments together in trying to create an atmosphere of better understanding.

We have said that India's problem is not poverty. If the SC/ST/BCs and Muslims are "poor", it is because the upper caste rulers have stolen our human rights. The moment we recover our human rights, we will become rich. So our problems are not poverty. Poverty-based struggle will mislead our people. The communist parties failed in India only because of this reason.

Unity with the Blacks

Q: Are you Dalits having any friends and allies abroad?

A: The Afro-American community in USA (Blacks) and other parts of the world are our best friends and we both suffer from the same identical racist aggression. This is my message that the necessity of the Dalit and Black unity is in the interests of both, not only to get rid of our burden but prevent another world war. This unity of the Dalits and Blacks will give our struggle a type of strength in spirit that will enable us to make some real concrete progress. We have to learn a lot from the Black struggle. They are at least 200 years ahead of us. In South Africa, they have taken to armed struggle. In US, they bid good-bye to nonviolence. Blacks are our own brothers and sisters. The African Blacks and Indian Black Untouchables have a common origin. There is nothing wrong in following the footsteps of our more advanced sisters and brothers. Hence the necessity of us forming a coalition, a working community with our brothers and sisters of the African continent and Afro-Americans.

For details read our book published in USA, *Dalit — The Black Untouchables of India* (Clarity Press, Atlanta, 1995).

Hate-mongering

Q: Why don't you preach love instead of hate?

A: If you go through the Brahmin religious texts you will know who is preaching hatred against whom. The most famous hate-teachers are Chanakya and Manu. But our (Dalit) literature, our speeches and writings have no proof of hate. Can you point out one person who is preaching hate?

The hate-mongers have stepped up their attack on the victims of their hatred. By violence they only mean that when a Black Dalit protects himself against the attacks of an upper caste man. This is what they mean by violence. They don't want you to defend yourself. They don't want us to protest. They don't want us to explode when they burn our huts. When the time comes for a Dalit man to explode, they call it violence. But the upper castes go on rampaging against our people all day long when they kick, kill, burn, rape and destroy our little property. That is never called violence. Are we for violence? Have we ever kicked, killed, burnt, raped or destroyed the properties of Hindus? Did we kill M.K. Gandhi, the Father of their nation? We are not merely the victims of violence, we are not merely the beasts of burden but we are also the beasts of prey. We have been so much victimised, persecuted that we have ceased to have pain. We can't even cry. The tears in our eyes have dried up.

An extremist ?

Q: You are an extremist. A terrorist. No wonder you were arrested under the Terrorist Act (1986).

A: I am often being dubbed an extremist. Yes. I proudly admit this charge. My reason for believing in extremism, intelligently directed extremism, extremism in defence of liberty, extremism in quest of justice is this: I am fully convinced that extremism has to be met with extremism. The day the Dalit takes an uncompromising step and realises that he is within his rights, when his own freedom is being threatened, to use any means necessary to bring about his freedom or put a halt to that injustice, I don't think he will be by himself. The Brahmins took to extremism to destroy Budhism. Did they not give up beef-eating and took to vegetarianism? Such an extremism, making a supreme sacrifice, is unknown in the history of the world. So we have any number of instances in history that extremism can be defeated only by extremism.

The 200 and odd million Dalits of India are yet to get angry and start hating the hate-teachers. Nor have they the desire for vengeance as the Brahminical propaganda would have you believe. If the upper caste oppressors had made our people even 10% angry, by this time the oppressors would have been blasted off, decimated. Most "intelligent" upper castes will admit without hesitation that they are already being punished for the evil deeds committed against the Dalits by their forefathers. Thus it is not necessary for the victim - the Dalits - to be vengeful. The very conditions the *savarnas*/ Aryans/upper castes/Hindus created are already plaguing them, haunting them into insanity and death. They are reaping what they have sown. We, the 200 and odd millions Dalits—the Black Untouchables, the victims — will do better to spend our time removing the scars from our people, the scar left by 4,000 years of inhuman treatment in India.

Women's liberation

Q: Does Dalit liberation include liberation of Dalit women?

A: The progress of any society or a country is to be judged by the progress made by its women who form 50% of its population. If you are in a country that can be called "progressive", its women must be fully free and liberated. If you are in a country that reflects the consciousness toward the importance of education, it is because the woman is aware of the importance of education. But in every backward society you will find the women also are backward. And in every society where education is not stressed, it is because the women don't have education. So one of the things I became thoroughly convinced of in my travels particularly China is the importance of freedom to the women.

Dalit movement is male-dominated

There is no work which a woman cannot do. In fact, she can do it better than man. I saw this in China and I was extremely happy. But our Brahminical Social Order does not believe in giving freedom to the woman. Even their own Brahmin women. We Dalits should not copy this from Hindus. Educating a boy is educating an individual. But educating a girl is educating a whole family. I am proud of the contributions that our Dalit women have made in the struggle for freedom and I am all for giving them all the leeway possible because they have made a greater contribution than many of us men.

I have to frankly admit that our men have started imitating the Hindu society and started tormenting their women. I find Dalit meetings are a mere male monopoly. Women are seldom brought to our meetings. They are seldom exposed to Ambedkarism. This has already done a great damage to the Dalit movement which is fully male-dominated. Woman is the maker and builder of a house because the mother has greater influence on her kids than the father. So, if the mother becomes an Ambedkarite, all her children will become Ambedkarites.

So remember, women's liberation is an essential part of the Dalit movement.

Self-hatred

Q: Your writings and speeches will be better appreciated if you stop preaching hatred. If you are less bitter.

A: Some upper caste journalists have the audacity to refer to me as a hate–teacher. If I am teaching someone to hate, I am only teaching them to hate only the Hindu terrorists. Not the Hindu society. But here in India our Hindu oppressors are teaching us to hate ourselves. Self-hatred is injected into our blood. To hate our skin, to hate our hair, to hate our features, to hate our blood, to hate our parents, to hate our ancestors, to hate our food. Hate what we are. This is called self-hatred.

The Brahminical scriptures are master hate–teachers. If you study these scriptures it will make us think that they are teaching us love while actually it is teaching us hate. When you have made a man hate himself then your job is done. Without arms you have won the battle. The enemy kills himself. You need not kill him. The Brahminical Social Order has destroyed our personality through self-hatred. So who is the hate teacher?

And, in my opinion, the young generation all over the world has been now living at a time of extremism, a time of revolution, a time when there has got to be a change. People, whether it be Hindus, Whites or Jews, in power have misused the power. Youth everywhere is fighting for a change and a better world has to be built. And the only way it is going to be built is with extreme methods. I for one will join with anyone, I don't care what colour you are, as long as you want to change this miserable condition that exists on this earth.

I don't care what you say about me. The world will judge me by my words and deeds. My life is an open book. The history has already pronounced its verdict.

What my biography says

Look what my biography (Kannada language) written by a Dalit scholar says (Rajendra, *Thereyannu Teredaga*, Ambedkar Pratishtana, 2005). Brother Rajendra, who spent days taking notes, nowhere says I preach hatred. He calls me a great humanist and a perfect student and disciple of Dr. Babasaheb Ambedkar.

Role of English language

Q: What do you say on learning English language?

A: This is a good question. In pre-independence days the Brahmins were refusing to teach us Sanskrit saying the *Deva Bhasha* (god's own language) is not meant for the people of the gutter but reserved for the heaven-born. But today the same Brahmins have deserted Sanskrit having taken to English but forcing the *Deva Bhasha* on us. Is this not a conspiracy to deny us the benefit of the international language which is the only window to the world? English today has become the world language and the Brahmin has mastered it and bagged the best of jobs. But injecting a mother tongue mania in us, he has made our people second class if not third class citizens. Our boys and girls by mastering their mother tongue at best can become clerks. Our youth should not fall prey to Brahminical tricks but master

English even while being good in mother tongue or else they will fail in this race. Once again the Brahmins can enforce slavery by denying us English knowledge. The government must make English compulsory right from first standard or even before that.

British rule

Q: How do you rate the British rule?

A: My father was a great admirer of British rule and the English language. He was telling me that it was the British who introduced education system which was reserved only for the Brahmins until then. They brought us postal system, railways, land records and more than anything the justice system which said that in the eyes of law every citizen is equal. The *Bhoodevatas* (Brahmins) lost half their power because of the British judicial system and Dalits for the first time got a just civil society.

It is the British rule that produced Dr. Ambedkar and gave us a Messiah. Should we not be grateful to the British? It is Gandhi and the Brahminical rulers who were the best slaves of the British and took the best advantage of the British as long as the British ruled India. It is only after 1947, they started saying that the British rule harmed India. Both the British and Muslim rule did so much of good to India. The Brahmin rule that we are now suffering since 1947 is the cause of our enslavement.

Q: Hindus say Muslims are terrorists. What do you say?

A: In *Dalit Voice*, at least 20% of our family members are Muslims. We have the closest relationship with Muslims. But we did not find any terrorist among them. The country's most ancient and the deadliest terrorists are the Brahminical people. Their Rashtriya Swayamsevak Sangh (RSS) is the country's most famous terrorist organisation. There is no such organisation among Muslims.

Islam as antidote

The Brahminical people use the terrorist label against Muslims to brainwash our innocent people and then instigate them against Muslims. They hate Muslims because their religion of Islam is the exact opposite to their Brahminical religion of graded inequality and racism. Thousands of innocent Muslims are today rotting in jails for years without even a single charge against them because of the Brahminical rule over India. Our judiciary and particularly the higher judiciary is totally Brahminical.

Muslims are our best and closest brothers. Over 85% of Indian Muslims are converts from SC/ST/BCs. Hence they are our blood brothers. Our people and Muslims live together. Both are beef-eaters. Nowhere in India we have any instance of Dalit-Muslim clash — except where there is clear instigation from the Brahminical terrorist organisations. Muslims are a vital part of the Bahujan Samaj. They are our elder brothers and our closest allies in our joint struggle against the BSO.

Q: When you are a Budhist, why are you advocating Islam?

A: This is a Brahminical false allegation. If I am advocating Islam, I should have become a Muslim not Budhist. If you have read our writings in *Dalit Voice* and heard our speeches at Muslim gatherings you will know that we are the bitterest critics of Muslim leadership, I mean the elite Muslims. Many of our speeches made at Muslim gatherings are published in DV or as a booklet. If we are advocating conversion to Islam, how we can afford to criticise Muslims?

Islam is the antidote to kill the poison of Brahminism. That is inside India. But in the West, Islam is fighting the White Western racist Christians and their zionist masters. In the US aggression of Afghanistan, Iraq and the war in Palestine, we have consistently supported Muslims because they have suffered under these aggression. We have also predicted that in this clash of religions (civilisation), Islam will come out victorious.

Judiciary

Q: You have been very critical of the higher judiciary, please explain.

A: Judiciary has been our biggest obstacle to social justice. Our governments, whether the Central or the States, are not so much opposed to social justice because a large number of elected representatives (MPs and MLAs) are our people. But those in the higher judiciary (judges) are not elected. They are appointed.

Mostly the Brahmins and other upper castes have monopolised the higher judiciary proving to be the worst enemies of Dalits, BCs, Muslims and all other weaker sections. We need to urgently overhaul this judiciary.

The Govt. of India must take over the power of appointing judges and also enforce reservation in higher judiciary. There is too much of corruption in higher judiciary.

Our deprived people all over India must also launch an agitation for this. Supreme Court is not supreme. The people are supreme. We need not fear the courts. They are creatures of the Constitution. When the Constitution itself is amended over 100 times, we can amend the Supreme Court also. The people have the power. Sovereignty lies with the people.

The Brahminical people with the support of their monopoly media are trying to disturb, destabilise and destroy our parliamentary democracy itself and its elected representatives with the help of this higher judiciary. We have warned the Supreme Court many times and we are sure it will take note of this warning seriously. (*Judicial Terrorism*, V.T. Rajshekar & Iqbal Ahmad Shariff, DSA-2006).

Swami Vivekananda ridiculed

Q: Brahmins are also human beings. Why do you hate them?

A: There is not a single instance in the thousands of years of Indian history of the Dalits hating Brahmins. We are the victims of their hatred. Dr. Ambedkar himself was a victim of Brahmin hatred. I was also a victim of Brahmin hatred. I was put in jail under TADA, my passport impounded for 20 long years. Two attempts on my life. Who hated whom? Can you get one Brahmin in the whole of India to testify that we hated him?

Gandhi loved Brahmins, made a Brahmin as India's first Prime Minister after getting "independence" for them to rule India. Why did they kill such a great lover of Brahmins?

Why did they ridicule Vivekananda as a *shudra* and dismissed him with the lowest and the meanest title of *swami* ?

We want to make it clear once for all that we have nothing against any individual Brahmin. Our criticism is only against Brahminism. Gandhi was not a Brahmin. Vivekananda was not a Brahmin. Yet we criticise both. We have criticised many people who are not Brahmins because their thinking was Brahminical. We hate Brahminism which is the other word for inhumanity, racism, unjust social order.

Individual Brahmin not hated

Dalits are ready to assure Brahmins full reservation in proportion to their population. May be a little more. But we will not allow them to run away with the existing over 50% reservation though their population is mere 3%.

Let me repeat: We hate no individual Brahmin. We hate the institution of Brahminism. But it must be also noted that there is no Brahminism without the Brahmin. If there is any good, honest Brahmin ready to fight Brahminism we are ready to embrace him. This question of a "good Brahmin" was answered by Periyar E.V. Ramaswamy when Gandhi asked him. Hence we don't want to repeat it here.

Jews & Hitler

Q: Of late you have written a lot on the hated Hitler

and criticised the zionists. In what way we Indians are concerned with these issues?

A: This is a good question. No human being can remain an island in today's world which has become a global village.

Like everybody else, I was also thinking that Hitler was a tyrant, a killer. But my later study, discussions and travels gave me a different picture. After Brother Iqbal Ahmed Shariff article came in DV (DV June 1, 2005 p.13: "*Brighter side of Hitler: DV to reveal facts suppressed by history*"), we got an entirely new picture of Hitler and his holocaust which proved to be a big bundle of lies.

Zionists supported Hitler

Alan Hart, a British Christian journalist of the BBC, has written a voluminous book, *Zionism — the Real Enemy of the Jews* (2005, World Focus Publishing, Kent, England) in which he speaks of the zionist terrorist support to Hitler. They first supported Mussolini of Italy and then Hitler of Germany (p.185). There was a perfect alliance of Jews and nazis. Hitler no doubt killed some Jews for their criminal behaviour but the holocaust as it is pictured later is a very exaggerated publicity build-up to bend Britain and later America and then control both the countries in which they fully succeeded.

The illegal occupation of Palestine belonging to Arabs is condemned by the United Nations itself. The havoc played by the 3% Jews in USA is now known to the whole world. And also the control of the entire world media, entertainment, finance and banking and through that politics and the governments. Read the shocking book of a famous American personality Henry Ford called *International Jew* (http://www.biblebelievers.org/au/intern_jew.htm).

The American attack on Afghanistan, followed by the attack on Iraq are at the instigation of zionists to protect their illegal occupation of Israel. Hitler's description of Jews and our calling Brahmin as the "Jews of India" gives the same picture.

All these are historical facts and DV has proved right.

DV proves right

Q: As we go through DV, now and then we are struck by your claim of "DV proves right". Do you say your claims are honest and truthful?

A: Our claims made in *Dalit Voice* are not oral but in black and white. Those who read our paper can challenge it and prove us wrong. The ever alert Brahminical people are examining every word of DV with the help of their magnifying glass. Our Website has thousands of readers, most of them Brahmins. Till this day nobody has told us that we are writing falsehood. DV will always prove right because we are always supporters of Justice and Truth and guided by Justice and Truth.

Principal contradiction

Q: What is the principal contradiction in India?

A: This is an important question because the Brahminical rulers with the help of their monopoly media have created too much of confusion by projecting all sorts of enemies to the oppressed to divert their attention from the principal enemy. Muslims are called the enemy No.1 of India "because they are terrorists". Communists point out the capitalists and landlords. Some others say it is globalisation. Many more enemies are named to confuse our people.

The confusion is deliberately created to divert their attention from Brahminism so that their energies are dissipated in fighting on different fronts and the real enemy that is hiding beneath is safe.

All these confusions are created by none other than our ruling class, the votaries of Brahminism, which is the principal contradiction.

To fight this deadliest enemy, all the victims of Brahminism, namely SC/ST/BCs and Muslim/Christian/Sikhs, will have to bend all their energies and work with a single-minded devotion. But Brahminism will not allow it because they control the media, our education system and history books and through that our brains. That is why the "struggle" launched by all the oppressed for justice becomes a waste and the real enemy is safe. In many cases it is the Brahmin himself who is "leading" the "struggle" of oppressed.

Anti-Brahmin war began with Budha

Right from the beginning of history the fight was only against the Brahmins and their Brahminism. Budha, the greatest of all Indians, fought only against Brahmins. So too all other revolutionaries down to Dr. Ambedkar. All of them had identified only one enemy — Brahminism. This is our historically proved principal contradiction. And we too are continuing this historical war.

The only problem facing us in launching such a war is the Muslims who have not yet identified the enemy. The masses of Muslims know the enemy but their elite religious and political leadership is hiding the truth and misleading the Muslim masses. But lately the Muslim masses have defied their leadership and started fighting Brahminism directly.

Had the Muslim leadership identified the enemy and named the enemy, our task would have been very easy because the Muslim population being 15% and we are 20%, the combined strength of the two would have simply scared the enemy.

Internal enemies

Q: Have you enemies within your ranks?

A: A person who fails to identify the principal contradiction is not only dishonest but also our enemy.

Yes. Such persons can't be trusted even if they are Dalits. Being thick in the Dalit struggle, we have come across many elite Dalits who have married Brahmin girls or occupying high positions by the grace of Brahmins or those Dalits in the NGO movement. The number of such stooges is increasing and right from the capital city of Delhi to every taluka headquarters the Brahmins have manufactured and planted one such SC/St/BC or Muslim/Christian/Sikh stooge. They have given him or her enough publicity, and made him/her as the "leader". Such stooges are given awards and rewards and offered good positions so that the oppressed, innocent Bahujans are overawed and silenced.

The best example is Jagjivan Ram, a creation of

Brahmins, but this poor man despite all the Brahmin blessings did not get any space in the Dalit heart. All such stooges die unsung and unwept by their own people.

Such stooges groomed by the Brahmins have no record of suffering or sacrifice. Their pictures very often appear in the press and their stupid speeches get yards and yards of coverage in the toilet papers. They are projected as models and used by the Brahmins to criticise those Dalits who have suffered and sacrificed. They are projected as the best model to the society. They make lot of noise but their contribution to Dalit liberation is nil. All their meetings are attended only by their upper caste admirers but genuine Dalit revolutionaries simply ignore them.

Though they are our own people and we don't to like criticise our own people, still to see that innocent Dalits do not fall into their net we have to sometimes break the tradition with sorrow.

Hiding the enemy

Though their impact on the society is nil, we can't spare them because their greatest sin is they are dishonest to their own people, society. Our Father, Dr. Ambedkar, has **identified** the enemy and **named** it as Brahminism. But these stooges are so dishonest that they hide the enemy by never naming the enemy. A Dalit leader or intellectual who is dishonest to Dr. Ambedkar is a dangerous enemy of the society because he is shielding the enemy. Such stooges even if they are our people have to be mercilessly exposed.

Internal contradictions are more dangerous than external ones. By keeping such internal contradictions in the society, our fight against the external (principal) contradiction becomes weaker. Hence the internal enemy has to be mercilessly exposed and fought. (Read Mao's book, *On Contradictions*).

Such stooges are there in plenty in all political parties particularly the *Brahmana Jati Party* (BJP). But all those Dalit, Tribal, BC and Muslim stooges who join the enemy will be ultimately made to eat dust. Their names become mud. They may get name, fame and money but ultimately lose the love of their people.

Double-peg brandy

These stooges easily fall into the Brahminical net because they get enamoured by the publicity they get in the media. Media publicity produces more intoxication than a double-peg brandy. Since the Brahmins control the media they can lavish any amount of publicity and thereby convert any donkey into a Derby race horse. But a real race horse is called a donkey. They tried to do it with Dr. Ambedkar. He spurned all such temptations and thereby conquered the hearts of all Dalits and also right thinking people of all castes and communities and came to be hailed as the "Father of India" — the highest title that anybody could get.

Remember, all those international awards instituted by Jews have to be cleared by the "Jews of India" before getting such awards in India. Even Naipaul, a Brahmin, was denied the Nobel Prize for literature for being critical of Brahmins in his early books. All those Indian award-winners have to be admirers of M.K. Gandhi, the Enemy no.1 of Dalits , Muslims, the entire Bahujans. Those given such national and international awards are projected as role models for their respective community and paraded. The whole intention is to kill the revolutionary zeal in Dalits and to see that they don't emulate Dr. Ambedkar. All those award-winners consider me and *Dalit Voice* as their enemy no.1. Dalits are told to always avoid us.

The simple test is why all the enemies of Dalits are praising these award-winners but criticising us?

Stooges

Those stooges on the Brahminical pay roll never identify the principal enemy. In fact they are praised and paraded only because they have the capacity to mislead the masses by hiding the real enemy. Such persons are not only dishonest but enemies of the Bahujans. Traitors to our society. Their names will never go into history. Only the toilet papers will carry their names. Brahmins have kept such stooges ready in every city to frighten us. Beware of such stooges. They will die a miserable death — cursed by their own society and silently laughed at by the upper castes. Their list is too long.

Q: You say only the Brahmins are so much hated by every section in India but not anybody else, why?

A: That Brahminism is our principal enemy is a historical fact. I have elaborated it in my book, *Brahminism* (DSA-2001). Brahmins are not the only foreign element in India. The Kshatriyas and Vaishyas (Gandhi's *jati*) too are foreigners and Aryans. Even the Jats are a foreign element. But none of them is hated. In Bihar, the Banias (Vaishyas) belong to the Backward Caste. Dr. R.M. Lohia was a Bania and yet he was responsible for launching a movement for Backward Castes in the Hindi belt.

Gandhi was a Gujarati Bania but in spite of his monumental service to Brahmins and handing over the country to Brahmins, finally it was only a Brahmin who killed Gandhi. (V.T. Rajshekar, *Why Godse Killed Gandhi?*, DSA–1997).

Though the Kshatriys are also Aryans, the Brahmin Parushuram killed all the Kshatriyas of the "world" as per the Brahmin legend. That is why the Kshatriyas (today called Thakurs) also hate Brahmins. V.P. Singh and Arjun Singh, both Thakurs, are hated by the Brahmins.

There is not a single revolutionary person who has not identified the Brahmin as the enemy of the entire oppressed Indians. Please go through the writings of all the Sikh gurus and Guru Ravidas. Even the Brahmin Basaveshwara of Karnataka (12th century) pointed out only one enemy. So also Mahatma Phule, Sri Narayana Guru, Sahu Maharaj, Periyar E.V. Ramasawamy and finally Dr. Ambedkar.

DV stand is time-tested

Even Swami Vivekananda, the high priest of Brahminism, has identified the Brahmin as the enemy of the country. (Swami Vivkananda, *Caste, Culture & Socialism*, Advaita Ashram, Calcutta, 1988). All the Backward Class commission, Scheduled Caste Commission reports of the Govt. of India and state governments have pointed their fingers at the Brahmins as the villain

Does it mean all these people were bloody fools? Those who pointed out and named the principal enemy of India are not ordinary people but the greatest revolutionaries whose names have gone into history and whose names are repeated and revered every day by millions even to this day.

In *Dalit Voice* and all my writings I have only followed the path shown by these revolutionaries and particularly the "Father of India", Dr. Babasaheb Ambedkar.

Our time-tested stand therefore is historically correct and based on our day-to-day experience in our socio-cultural movement.

Message of hate

Q: Brahmins say that *Dalit Vice* from beginning to end has nothing but one message: the message of hate. The Brahmins after all are a mere 3% of India's vast 1,000-odd million population. How can such a small population be capable of tyrannising the 97% of its people? Brahmins are the country's most learned people and its intellectual class. Definitely they can be won over by convincing them and promoting a change of heart in them but certainly not through endless hate-mongering.

A: We have answered this question in *Dalit Voice* many times by using the words of Dr. Ambedkar himself and America's great Black leader, Stokely Carmichael (DV May 16, 2006 p.24: "*In defence of polemics*"). Yet it needs repetition.

I want to reply in the words of Menachem Begin, a top

zionist world leader who later became the Prime Minister of Israel and awarded a Nobel Peace Prize.

We have called the Brahmins as the "Jews of India". And they have gladly accepted this description.

India had never recognised Israel but it was under a Brahmin Prime Minister, P.V. Narasimha Rao, India recognised it and the *Brahmana Jati Party* (BJP) that succeed became Israel's soul-mate. India's ruling class forced India to become a tail of America at the instance of the zionists. So naturally to such of the Brahminical people what Begin says must be a *Veda Vakya* (god's own words).

Menachem Begin was a world class Jew once holding the highest position as the Prime Minister and Nobel laureate. He wrote a book, *The Revolt* (Nash Publishing, Los Angeles, 1972, p.xii).

We have taken the quotation from the book of Alan Hart, *Zionism — The Real Enemy of the Jews*, 2005, World Focus Publishing, Kent, England).

As the Brahmins and the zionists think alike and act alike and have created the same situation, Begin's reply to the "message of hate" alone can convince our critics instead of quoting from Dr. Ambedkar:

If you don't hate, you can't love

> It is axiomatic that those who have to fight have to hate something or somebody. And we fought. We had to hate first and foremost the horrifying, age-old, inexcusable utter defenselessness of our Jewish people, wandering through millennia, through a cruel world, to the majority of whose inhabitants the defenselessness

> of the Jews was a standing invitation to massacre them. We had to hate the humiliating disgrace of the homelessness of our people. We had to hate — as any nation worthy of the name must and always will hate — the rule of the foreigner, rule unjust and unjustifiable per se, foreign rule in the land of our ancestors, in our own country. We had to hate the barring of our gates of our own country to our own brethren, trampled and bleeding and crying out for help in a world morally deaf. And, naturally, we had to hate all those who, equipped with modern arms and with the ancient machinery of the gallows, barred the way of our people to physical salvation, denied them of the means of individual defence, frustrated their efforts for national independence and ruthlessly withstood their attempts to regain their national honour and restore their self respect... Who will condemn the hatred of evil that springs from the love of what is good and just? (p. 189-190).

Begin's above reply to the question why the Jews hate the Palestinian Muslims — that produced over 100-year-old world's longest lasting problem — sums up the answer to the charge that *Dalit Voice* is "message of hate".

For every action there has to be a reaction. This is a dialectical philosophy. Every emotion has an opposition emotion. Brahminical scriptures, gods and their Brahminical Social Order continues to hate us and inflicted the worst violence on our people. Since we love our people we have to hate those who hate us. If you don't hate you can't love — unless you are one-sided.

Menachem Begin is described by Alan Hart as "the most

successful terrorist leader of modern times" (p.188). India's premier Brahminical terrorist party, RSS-BJP, has the closest connection with Israel and zionists and as such the Brahminical people of India cannot find a better answer to their question than in the words of their own blood brother as well as a hero.

The simple point Menachem Begin makes here is all those who love their people also have to hate the people who oppress them.

This is also our answer to our critics saying we are spreading a message of hate.